BRITISH RAILWAYS STEAMING THROUGH THE MIDLANDS

Volume One

Compiled by
PETER HANDS

DEFIANT PUBLICATIONS
190 Yoxall Road
Shirley, Solihull
West Midlands

Printed on behalf of Richard Netherwood Limited., by Gorenjski tisk p.o., Kranj, Slovenia

CURRENT STEAM PHOTOGRAPH ALBUMS AVAILABLE
FROM DEFIANT PUBLICATIONS

BRITISH RAILWAYS STEAMING THROUGH THE SIXTIES

VOLUME 14
A4 size - Hardback. 96 pages -178 b/w photographs.
£14.95 + £1.50 postage.
ISBN 0 946857 40 7.

BRITISH RAILWAYS STEAMING THROUGH THE SIXTIES

IN PREPARATION

VOLUME 15

BRITISH RAILWAYS STEAMING THROUGH THE SIXTIES

IN PREPARATION

VOLUME 16

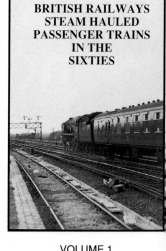

BRITISH RAILWAYS STEAM HAULED PASSENGER TRAINS IN THE SIXTIES

VOLUME 1
A4 size - Hardback. 96 pages -177 b/w photographs.
£14.95 + £1.50 postage.
ISBN 0 946857 41 5.

BRITISH RAILWAYS STEAMING THROUGH THE FIFTIES

VOLUME 9
A4 size - Hardback. 96 pages -177 b/w photographs.
£14.95 + £1.50 postage.
ISBN 0 946857 37 7.

BRITISH RAILWAYS STEAMING THROUGH THE FIFTIES

VOLUME 10
A4 size - Hardback. 96 pages -176 b/w photographs.
£14.95 + £1.50 postage.
ISBN 0 946857 38 5.

BRITISH RAILWAYS STEAMING THROUGH THE FIFTIES

IN PREPARATION

VOLUME 11

BRITISH RAILWAYS STEAMING THROUGH THE FIFTIES

IN PREPARATION

VOLUME 12

BRITISH RAILWAYS STEAM HAULED PASSENGER TRAINS IN THE FIFTIES

VOLUME 1
A4 size - Hardback. 96 pages -177 b/w photographs.
£14.95 + £1.50 postage.
ISBN 0 946857 39 3.

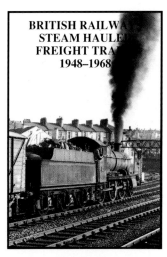

BRITISH RAILWAYS STEAM HAULED FREIGHT TRAINS 1948–1968

VOLUME 1
A4 size - Hardback. 96 pages -174 b/w photographs.
£14.95 + £1.50 postage.
ISBN 0 946857 42 3.

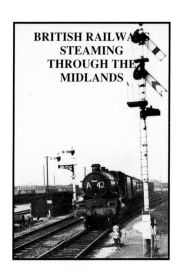

BRITISH RAILWAYS STEAMING THROUGH THE MIDLANDS

VOLUME 1
A4 size - Hardback. 96 pages -179 b/w photographs.
£15.95 + £1.50 postage.
ISBN 0 946857 43 I.

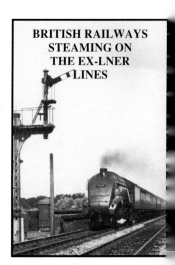

BRITISH RAILWAYS STEAMING ON THE EX-LNER LINES

VOLUME 3
A4 size - Hardback. 96 pages -183 b/w photographs.
£15.95 + £1.50 postage.
ISBN 0 946857 44 X.

FUTURE STEAM PHOTOGRAPH ALBUMS
AND OTHER TITLES

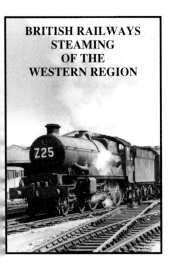

**BRITISH RAILWAYS
STEAMING
OF THE
WESTERN REGION**

VOLUME 4
OCTOBER 1994

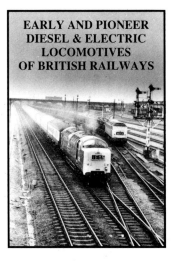

**EARLY AND PIONEER
DIESEL & ELECTRIC
LOCOMOTIVES
OF BRITISH RAILWAYS**

OCTOBER 1994

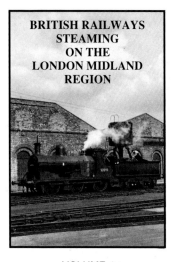

**BRITISH RAILWAYS
STEAMING
ON THE
LONDON MIDLAND
REGION**

VOLUME 4
OCTOBER 1994

**BRITISH RAILWAYS
STEAMING
ON THE
SOUTHERN REGION**

**IN
PREPARATION**

VOLUME 3

**STEAM HAULED
TITLED TRAINS
OF
BRITSH RAILWAYS**

**IN
PREPARATION**

VOLUME 1

**BRITISH RAILWAYS
STEAMING
THROUGH CREWE,
DONCASTER,
EASTLEIGH AND
SWINDON**

**IN
PREPARATION**

**BRITISH RAILWAYS
STEAMING
THROUGH LONDON**

**IN
PREPARATION**

**BRITISH RAILWAYS
STEAMING ON
THE EX-LNER
LINES**

**IN
PREPARATION**

VOLUME 4

**BRITISH RAILWAYS
STEAM HAULED
FREIGHT TRAINS
1948–1968**

**IN
PREPARATION**

VOLUME 2

**BRITISH RAILWAYS
STEAM HAULED
PASSENGER TRAINS
IN THE
FIFTIES**

**IN
PREPARATION**

VOLUME 2

**BRITISH RAILWAYS
STEAM HAULED
PASSENGER TRAINS
IN THE
SIXTIES**

**IN
PREPARATION**

VOLUME 2

It's a dog's life in the
FIRE SERVICE
by Peter St.Bernard

COMEDY
269 pages. Cartoons.
£9.95 + £1.00 postage.
ISBN 0 946857 30 X.

ACKNOWLEDGEMENTS

Grateful thanks are extended to the following contributors of photographs not only for their use in this book but for their kind patience and long term loan of negatives/photographs whilst this book was being compiled.

T.R.AMOS TAMWORTH	H.H.BLEADS BIRMINGHAM	B.W.L.BROOKSBANK LONDON
N.L.BROWNE ALDERSHOT	L.BROWNHILL KINGSWINFORD	R.S.CARPENTER BIRMINGHAM
J.K.CARTER MILLHOLME	A.R.CURTIS **	S.DARTNELL DERBY
J.DOWNING SOLIHULL	TIM FAREBROTHER BOURTON	J.D.GOMERSALL SHEFFIELD
A.N.H.GLOVER BIRMINGHAM	B. K. B. GREEN *	D.HARRISON CHAPELTOWN
PETER HAY HOVE	R.W.HINTON GLOUCESTER	F.HORNBY NORTH CHEAM
A.C.INGRAM WISBECH	L.C.JACKS BIRMINGHAM	D.K.JONES MOUNTAIN ASH
A.F.NISBET BRACKLEY	D.OAKES HITCHIN	M.PAINE KIDDERMINSTER
R.PICTON WOLVERHAMPTON	DON POWELL ****	N.E.PREEDY HUCCLECOTE
P.A.ROWLINGS ALCONBURY	J.SCHATZ LITTLETHORPE	K.L.SEAL ANDOVERSFORD
G.W.SHARPE BARNSLEY	J.M.TOLSON BIGGLESWADE	TERRY WARD NORTHAMPTON
D.WEBSTER ***	B.WILSON SOLIHULL	MIKE WOOD BIRMINGHAM

*   Courtesy of C.Stacey.
**   Courtesy of the A.C.Ingram collection.
***   Courtesy of the N.E.Preedy collection.
**** Courtesy of the R.S.Carpenter collection.

Front Cover – With the chalked train reporting number A42 spread across the smokebox door, 85A Worcester based GWR *Castle* Class 4-6-0 No 7005 *Sir Edward Elgar* approaches Honeybourne station under clear signals with a Worcester to Paddington express on 20th April 1961. (B. Wilson)

ISBN 0 946857 43 1

(C) P.B.HANDS 1994
FIRST PUBLISHED 1994

INTRODUCTION

BRITISH RAILWAYS STEAMING THROUGH THE MIDLANDS Volume One has been published in direct response to specific requests by a number of 'Defiant Publications' customers.

The author has attempted to vary the locations and types of locomotive classes within the pages of this album in order to please the varied interests of the readers. Some areas of greater interest, such as Birmingham, Derby, Gloucester, Leicester, Nottingham, Oxford, Rugby, Wolverhampton and Worcester have been given more coverage than others.

BRITISH RAILWAYS STEAMING THROUGH THE MIDLANDS – Volume One is divided into five chapters. The locations include large cities, industrial areas, huge Motive Power Depots, branch lines, country scenes and small, less well known sheds.

It is hoped that the reader will appreciate that it is difficult to pinpoint where the dividing lines are between the different regional areas. Hopefully the author has managed to create an enjoyable balance between these *grey* areas.

The 'BR Steaming' series of books are designed to give the ordinary, everyday steam photographic enthusiast of the 1950's and 1960's a chance to participate in and give pleasure to others whilst recapturing the twilight days of steam.

Apart from the 1950's and 1960's series, individual albums like this one will be produced from time to time. Wherever possible, no famous names will be found nor will photographs which have been published before be used. Nevertheless, the content and quality of the majority of photographs used will be second to none.

The majority of the photographs used in this album have been contributed by readers of Peter Hands series of booklets entitled 'What Happened to Steam' & 'BR Steam Shed Allocations' and from readers of the earlier 'BR Steaming Through the Sixties' albums. In normal circumstances these may have been hidden from the public eye for ever.

The continuation of the 'BR Steaming' series etc., depends upon *you* the reader. If you wish to join my direct mailing list for future albums and/or feel you have suitable material of BR steam locomotives between 1948–1968 and wish to contribute them towards the main series and other albums, please contact:

Tel No.
021 745-8421

Peter Hands
190 Yoxall Road,
Shirley, Solihull,
West Midlands B90 3RN

CONTENTS

CHAPTER	LOCATIONS	PAGES
ONE	BIRMINGHAM AREA	5–21
TWO	EAST MIDLANDS	22–39
THREE	NORTH MIDLANDS	40–57
FOUR	SOUTH MIDLANDS	58–75
FIVE	WEST MIDLANDS	76–94

CHAPTER ONE - BIRMINGHAM AREA

1) A panoramic view of Birmingham (New Street) station - circa 1959. In the left hand side of this print is the former LNWR section with the ex Midland Railway sector on the right. (Note the differences between the roof structures.) At this stage in time both stations are divided by Queen's Drive, but this thoroughfare disappeared after reconstruction in 1967. Today, New Street station is a characterless, concrete monolith. (R.S.Carpenter)

2) A terra firma view of the London & North Western section of Birmingham (New Street) as photographed from the Wolverhampton end of platforms 5/6. In the distance (right) just out of sight is Monument Lane Tunnel, whilst to the left we can just make out the entrance on the Midland side to the tunnel leading to Five Ways and beyond. A common feature of the LNWR side are the short, stubby upper quadrant signals (foreground). (L.Brownhill)

3) We remain within the confines of the former LNWR station at New Street, where, in April 1960, we espy two former LMS locomotives awaiting departure with northbound expresses. On the left is a locally based Class 5 4-6-0 No 44876 (3D Aston). Adjacent to No 44876 is *Jubilee* Class 4-6-0 No 45593 *Kolhapur*, from 12B Carlisle (Upperby). The latter engine is still with us, but No 44876 was cut up during March 1968. (H.H.Bleads)

4) With excess steam escaping from the safety valves, more steam is released from the cylinder cocks of LMS Class 5 4-6-0 No 45385, an inmate of 9A Longsight (Manchester), as it stands at the head of a relief express at the London end (LNWR) of Birmingham (New Street) in the summer of 1963. Transferred briefly to 26F Patricroft, No 45385 was destined to spend the last three years of its working life at 8F Springs Branch Wigan. (L.Brownhill)

5) We now turn our attentions to the Midland side of New Street, where it is semi-final day in the FA Cup on 27th April 1963. A lengthy football special packed with Southampton fans bound for Villa Park snakes its way into platform 7. A gaggle of photographers and spotters admire the graceful lines of a longstanding resident of 82E Bristol Barrow Road, LMS *Jubilee* Class 4-6-0 No 45682 *Trafalgar*, which is in charge of the special. (L.Brownhill)

6) Unlike the LNWR section of New Street, the former Midland Railway side boasted a large number of normal sized upper quadrant signals, like the ones in the left of this picture. Its tender filled to capacity, BR Class 5 4-6-0 No 73096 simmers gently at the head of the 12.15pm local passenger to Worcester on 7th August 1962. Allocated to 85C Gloucester (Barnwood) the previous month, No 73096 had for many years been at Shrewsbury shed. (J.Schatz)

7) We take our leave of Birmingham (New Street) and head northwards on former LNWR tracks. A listing (rather than listed!) building looks down on the railway scene at Soho and Winson Green station (Stour Valley Line) in the mid-fifties, where on the right there is a canal. Centrepiece of this photograph is 3B Bushbury (Wolverhampton) based LMS *Jubilee* Class 4-6-0 No 45734 *Meteor* which is in charge of a Wolverhampton (High Level) express. (R.S.Carpenter)

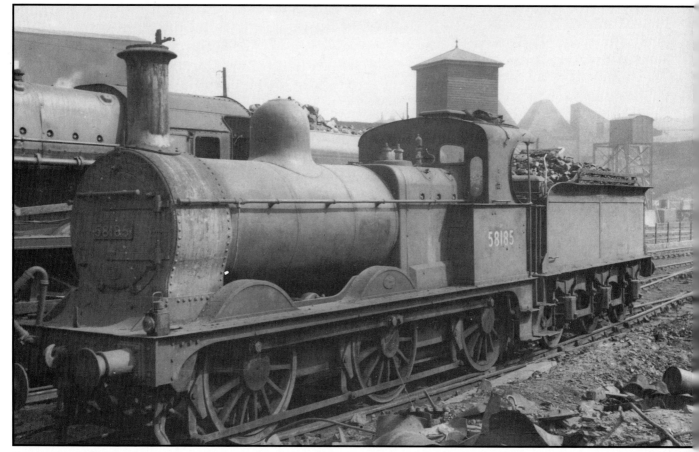

8) The nearest shed to Birmingham (New Street), on the northern side, was at Monument Lane, a short distance from the tunnel leading to New Street. Its allocation consisted of a mixture of classes, but few more elderly than the Johnson designed Class 2F 0-6-0's, the first examples of which were first introduced into service in 1875. 'On shed' at 3E in 1959 is No 58185, which lingered on in service until July 1962. (R.S.Carpenter)

9) Moving to a different route away from New Street station we find ourselves at Vauxhall. In the background are a conglomeration of structures - gasholders - grubby tenement dwellings and factory units. An unidentified LMS Tank locomotive stands near a seemingly endless rake of carriages as LMS Class 8F 2-8-0 No 48317, from 16B Kirkby, with steam to spare, threads a path with a heavily laden permanent way train in the mid-fifties. (R.S.Carpenter)

10) On a dismal summer's day in 1960, LMS Hughes 'Crab' Class 6P5F 2-6-0 No 42761 rounds a curve and approaches the site of Sutton Coldfield Town station, closed in 1925, with an up empty stock working. The tracks which No 42761 is traversing belongs to the route from Walsall-Sutton Park-Castle Bromwich (Midland Railway). No 42761, a long-term favourite at 21A Saltley, moved to pastures new at 9G Gorton in June 1961. (R.S.Carpenter)

11) Another depot which supplied steam locomotives for services to and from Birmingham (New Street) was at Aston (closed in October 1965). Sixteen years earlier the spectre of closure was a far off nightmare to the shed staff at Aston. In the shed yard at 3D on 13th August 1949 is a visitor from 19B Millhouses in the shape of LMS Class 5 4-6-0 No 45450 which is departing from the depot to take up a local working. (A.N.H.Glover)

12) Also captured on camera on the same day at Aston shed is locally based LMS Class 4 2-6-4T No 42538 and LMS Class 6P5F 2-6-0 No 42960. Despite some twenty months having passed since nationalisation No 42960 is still carrying the cabside numerals of 2960. Although No 42538 spent its working life on the London Midland Region, for reasons best known to the authorities it was transferred to 33C Shoeburyness in June 1962 and then withdrawn. (A.N.H.Glover)

3) Moving away from Aston shed, the next location is at Bromford Bridge station, once the drop-off point for punters visiting the long since demised Birmingham Racecourse, on the main line from New Street to Derby. On 5th September 1962, LMS *Jubilee* Class 4-6-0 No 45668 *Madden*, from 17B Burton, rattles through Bromford Bridge with a down Class 9 mineral freight. The external condition of *Madden* leaves a lot to be desired. (B.W.L.Brooksbank)

4) The final shed which supplied locomotives to New Street, mainly on the former Midland Railway section, is at Saltley, coded 21A and finally 2E. On the turntable in the 'open' roundhouse on a misty February day in 1960 is a visitor from 84E Tyseley, GWR *Hall* Class 4-6-0 No 5912 *Queen's Hall*. Looking on are a trio of LMS Class 5 4-6-0's Nos 44660, 44888, 44775 and a solitary BR Class 9F 2-10-0 No 92137. (R.S.Carpenter)

15) Despite ample space within the large roundhouses at Saltley the yard was a rather confined place and at times of maximum occupation, usually a Sunday, there was little spare capacity. Hemmed between two locomotives, 20B Normanton based LMS Class 4F 0-6-0 No 44604 sports the logo of its owner on its high-sided tender as it rests between duties on 13th August 1949. Records show that No 44604 stayed at Normanton until January 1964. (A.N.H.Glover)

16) The photographer has moved on to a different section of the yard at Saltley on 13th August 1949 and captures for posterity a picture of a locally based former Midland Railway Class 3F 0-6-0 No 43673, yet another engine sporting the lettering of its former owner and numerals without the prefix (4). Used in the main on banking duties and local freight workings, No 43673 was condemned from Saltley in September 1961. (A.N.H.Glover)

7) To ease congestion through Birmingham (New Street) a relief line was built by the Midland Railway which basically ran from St.Andrews Junction to Lifford, being used in the main by freight traffic supplemented by through excursion passenger trains. In April 1960, former Midland Railway Class 4F 0-6-0 No 43951, from 21A Saltley, struggles through the closed Kings Heath station with a mixed freight bound for Bromsgrove. (H.H.Bleads)

8) A closer view of Kings Heath station complete with the small signalbox in October 1948. (Note the tricycle on view.) Another 21A Saltley based freight locomotive, LMS Class 8F 2-8-0 No 48388 hurries a southbound freight through the station. Kings Heath station, along with the other intermediate stations on this route, Hazelwell, Moseley and Camp Hill were closed by the Midland Railway during 1941. (H.H.Bleads)

19) We now switch our attentions to the former Great Western Railway lines around Birmingham and find ourselves at Snow Hill station the main rival to New Street. Unlike New Street station quite a large proportion of trains running through Snow Hill were of the freight variety. Watched by a small band of travellers, GWR 2800 Class 2-8-0 No 3846 (89B Croes Newydd) heads a down iron-ore train on a misty 3rd November 1962. (J.Schatz)

20) On an unknown, but bright day in 1958, GWR *Hall* Class 4-6-0 No 4964 *Rodwell Hall*, from 84C Banbury, awaits signals whilst on a through road at the northern end of Snow Hill. In the background we can see the oddly shaped power signalbox which was soon to spell the death knell of the two manual boxes employed at Snow Hill. In July 1962 *Rodwell Hall* was drafted to a new home at 84A Wolverhampton (Stafford Road). (R.S.Carpenter)

21) A wintry setting at Snow Hill station with steam a'plenty highlighted by the crisp and cold conditions after a fall of snow in the winter of 1957. GWR 5100 Class 2-6-2T No 5110 supplies steam heating to the grateful passengers within the three coach local which it is preparing to haul to its home base at Kidderminster. During 1959 No 5110 found itself at Shrewsbury and Worcester sheds. It was withdrawn in December 1960. (R.S.Carpenter)

22) Some six weeks after the mighty GWR *King* Class 4-6-0's were withdrawn from express workings on the main Paddington to Birkenhead route and the dieselisation of the services, steam makes a comeback, albeit as a substitute for the rostered diesel. GWR *Castle* Class 4-6-0's Nos. 5089 *Westminster Abbey* and 7019 *Fowey Castle*, both from 84A Wolverhampton (Stafford Road) await departure from Snow Hill with an up express on 21st October 1962. (J.Schatz)

23) A cold and miserable winter's day in November 1957 greets the arrival of BR Class 3 2-6-2T No 82008 (85D Kidderminster) as it slips through the gap between the new and the old signalboxes at Snow Hill before gliding to a halt in a bay platform with a three coach local commuter train. Before being taken out of service in February 1964 No 82008 worked from depots as far apart as 85A Worcester, 89C Machynlleth, 87H Neyland and 83B Taunton. (R.S.Carpenter)

24) Another view of the northern end of Snow Hill, looking down the gradient to the short tunnel in the left background which leads to Hockley. 82C Swindon based BR Class 5 4-6-0 No 73020 heads a short express in an up direction into platform 7 in the mid to late fifties. Transferred to 71G Weymouth in October 1958, No 73020 was destined to spend the remainder of its working life on the Southern, being withdrawn in July 1967. (R.S.Carpenter)

25) This is the same location, but with a difference - note that the manual signalbox in the left of the previous picture has vanished, along with the semaphore signals in the frame. GWR *Grange* Class 4-6-0 No 6821 *Leaton Grange*, a visitor to Birmingham (Snow Hill) from 86G Pontypool Road, arrives from Hockley sidings and steams past the camera with a southbound empty coaching stock train (return excursion) in 1960. (R.S.Carpenter)

26) A final view of Birmingham (Snow Hill) looking towards the Paddington end of the station, on 17th November 1956. In charge of a down Class 8 freight on a through track is a far from home 86C Cardiff (Canton) based GWR 2800 Class 2-8-0 No 3809. Surplus to requirements at Canton shed in January 1961, No 3809 was moved to a new home at 84C Banbury. Its final allocation was to 6C Croes Newydd in April 1964 - withdrawn six months later. (D.K.Jones)

27) Under clear signals an ex. works GWR *Hall* Class 4-6-0 No 5977 *Beckford Hall*, from 85C Hereford, passes a signalbox at Soho & Winson Green station on the Birmingham (Snow Hill) to Wolverhampton (Low Level) main line in August 1956. Between June 1958 and February 1960, *Beckford Hall* served from Shrewsbury, Old Oak Common, Reading and Gloucester (Horton Road) sheds. Its last home was at 81D Reading from February 1960 to August 1963. (R.S.Carpenter)

28) Gaunt, cramped dwellings and an iron road bridge dominate the scene, again taken at Soho & Winson Green station, but this time on 19th July 1956. 82A Bristol (Bath Road) based GWR *Modified Hall* Class 4-6-0 No 7907 *Hart Hall* heads an express consisting of a rake of 'Blood & Custard' coaches towards the station which closed completely in 1972. *Hart Hall* demised seven years earlier, taken out of traffic in December 1965 from 81F Oxford. (D.K.Jones)

29) We track southwards from Snow Hill and find ourselves at Tyseley, where, during the summer of 1965 we spot BR Class 9F 2-10-0 No 92243, from 86B Newport (Ebbw Junction), in action at the head of a fitted freight. Introduced into service as late as October 1958, built at Crewe Works, No 92243 only had a short working life, being condemned in December 1965. Its poor external condition belies its strength and efficiency. (Tim Farebrother)

30) A thin scattering of passengers and a barrow load of packages are present on the platforms at Tyseley station as GWR 2800 Class 2-8-0 No 3834, allocated to 81C Southall, steams through with an up partially fitted goods train on a cold, 26th January 1963. Today, the station at Tyseley is a listed building and the nearby depot still supports steam. No 3834, alas, is no longer with us, cut up at Birds, Risca in February 1965. (M.Wood)

31) WD Austerity Class 8F 2-8-0 No 77380 (90268) sports a 'NOT TO BE MOVED' notice outside the entrance to the engine factory at 84E Tyseley on 22nd May 1949. This locomotive worked in France until 1946 and then worked from sheds on the Western Region until July 1962, when it was drafted to the LMR at 8F Springs Branch Wigan. From then on it remained on the LMR until condemned from 10H Lower Darwen in April 1965. (A.N.H.Glover)

32) The interior of Tyseley shed late one evening in 1964 when the depot carried the code of 2A. Present are two GWR *Grange* Class 4-6-0's and BR Class 9F 2-10-0 No 92215, a local engine. One *Grange* has lost its front numberplate, but No 6827 *Llanfrechfa Grange* (2C Stourbridge) is identifiable although in a filthy state. Born in February 1937 it was first shedded at 83F Truro. Withdrawal came from 2B Oxley in September 1965. (Tim Farebrother)

33) On Sunday 29th September 1963, 1A Willesden based LMS *Coronation* Class 4-6-2 No 46245 *City of London* was employed on a Warwickshire Railway Society special from Birmingham (Snow Hill) to Crewe and Shrewsbury. 5A Crewe (North), 5B Crewe (South), Crewe Works and 89A (6D) Shrewsbury were visited by the passengers and somewhere in excess of 230 steam locomotives were seen. *City of London* is seen here at rest in the yard at Tyseley after the journey. (Mike Wood)

34) We complete this pictorial quartet at Tyseley shed with a shot of one of its local inhabitants, BR Class 9F 2-10-0 No 92212, fresh from overhaul, on 30th August 1964 at rest in the yard. Constructed in late 1959, No 92212 served from Banbury, Bath Green Park, Newport (Ebbw Junction), Tyseley and Carnforth sheds before its premature withdrawal from the latter in January 1968. Today, it is alive and well in the hands of the preservationists. (D.Webster)

CHAPTER TWO - EAST MIDLANDS

35) We commence the East Midlands section with this action photograph of LMS Class 8F 2-8-0 No 48603, from 2E Saltley, which blasts its way along the upgrade with mineral wagons on 30th December 1966. No 48603 is passing the site of Kingsbury Colliery on the branch to Birch Coppice and Baddesley pits. When Saltley shed closed to steam in March 1967, No 48603 was drafted to 6A Chester. It was only a brief respite for it was withdrawn three months later. (T.R.Amos)

36) Powering an express freight, 12A Carlisle (Kingmoor) based LMS *Jubilee* Class 4-6-0 No 45588 *Kashmir* bursts from beneath Ashby Road bridge, near Tamworth and heads for Birmingham on 19th April 1963. Transferred to Carlisle (Upperby) from 24E Blackpool in October 1957, *Kashmir* was destined to remain in the Carlisle area until taken out of revenue earning service in May 1965. Motherwell Machinery & Scrap Co., claimed the remains. (T.R.Amos)

37) The same location, but in reverse, again taken on 19th April 1963. Bright sunshine envelopes LMS Class 2 2-6-0 No 46421, from 21B Bescot, as it chugs along with a 'mixed bag' of vehicles between Tamworth and Burton. Records show that from January 1957 at least, No 46421 was also allocated to Bescot. It had a brief foray at 21C Bushbury, June to August 1962, before returning to Bescot. Its final home was at 2E Saltley. (T.R.Amos)

38) Summer foliage waves about in the breeze caused by the passing of an express in July 1957. In charge of the unidentified passenger train at Kettlebrook is BR Class 5 4-6-0 No 73031, newly allocated to 82E Bristol Barrow Road from 17A Derby. In January 1958, No 73031 was sent to Rugby Testing Station and not released (according to records) until December 1961 when it was despatched to 82F Bath Green Park. (D.K.Jones)

39) Steam's eleventh hour on the West Coast Main Line at Nuneaton in April 1966. An unidentified LMS Ivatt Class 2 2-6-0, from the nearby shed at 5E Nuneaton, is in charge of a Railway Correspondence & Travel Society special. At this stage in time there were still four of these engines on Nuneaton's books - Nos 46495, 46512, 46519 and 46520. All were taken out of service when the shed closed to steam on 6th June 1966. (G.W.Sharpe)

40) Begrimed 16F Burton based LMS Class 8F 2-8-0 No 48332, minus shedplate, is a visitor to 5E Nuneaton on 11th July 1965. In this scene it appears that No 48332 is being employed on shed pilot duties near to the dilapidated coaling stage. For many years a Toton engine, No 48332 was allocated to Burton from May 1962 to June 1966. Between the latter date and withdrawal in October 1967 it worked from a further four depots. (N.E.Preedy)

41) LMS *Royal Scot* Class 4-6-0 No 46141 *The North Staffordshire Regiment*, allocated to 21A Saltley, suffers the indignity of being employed on a far more menial task than it was designed for. *The North Staffordshire Regiment* heads a train of loose-coupled mineral trucks out of Kingsbury Sidings in 1962. A later transfer, in July of the same year, saw No 46141 at 12B Carlisle (Upperby) where it survived until April 1964. (R.S.Carpenter)

42) The next photo-stop in 'BR Steaming Through the Midlands' is at Rugby where legions of spotters spent their youth in the days of steam. It is discussion time between members of the BR fraternity as BR Class 2 2-6-0 No 78063, newly transferred to 1A Willesden from 27D Wigan L & Y, steams and sizzles at the head of two vans in Rugby (Midland) station on 7th May 1963. (D.K.Jones)

43) 1962 proved to be last year that we could see the mighty LMS *Princess* Class 4-6-2's in normal active British Railways service. On a hot and sunny August day in 1962, No 46206 *Princess Marie Louise*, from 1B Camden, heads northwards out of Rugby (Midland) with a down empty stock working. For many years a 5A Crewe (North) locomotive, No 46206 also had brief spells at 2A Rugby. The end came in October 1962 from 1B Camden. (G.W.Sharpe)

4) South of Rugby (Midland) the tracks are spanned by lofty road bridges from where spotters and photographers alike could observe from on high the comings and goings of trains on this section of the West Coast Main Line. From one such vantage point we espy the passage of an up express on 23rd July 1960. In charge of this train is 21D Aston LMS *Jubilee* Class 4-6-0 No 45647 *Sturdee* which sports a 'stained' front end. (D.K.Jones)

5) The same photographer pans his camera round and points his lens in the direction of Rugby (Midland) on the same day and captures for posterity the passing of LMS *Royal Scot* Class 4-6-0 No 46100 *Royal Scot*, of 16A Nottingham, as it emerges from beneath a flyover and heads southwards with an up express. Withdrawn from 16A Nottingham in October 1962, *Royal Scot* currently resides at Bressingham Steam Museum in Norfolk. (D.K.Jones)

46) In its prime the depot at 2A Rugby was a massive structure which housed a large allocation within its straight running shed. It was also a hard place to 'bunk' as many spotters found out to their cost. On shed in early February 1962, next to an impressive water tower, is LMS *Royal Scot* Class 4-6-0 No 46154 *The Hussar*, a 6G Llandudno Junction steed, its footplate crew well wrapped up against the cold conditions. (G.W.Sharpe)

47) Fresh from overhaul at Crewe Works, LMS Class 5 4-6-0 No 44935 is a visitor to Rugby shed from 12A Carlisle (Kingmoor) in May 1963. This close-up of the running shed does little justice to the actual size of the place with its plethora of tracks. Very few named engines were based at Rugby, but those that were, were from within the ranks of the LMS *Jubilee* and *Patriot* classes, the odd *Princess* and BR *Britannia's*. (G.W.Sharpe)

48) We switch tracks from the former London & North Western Railway to those of the Great Central at Rugby, where, by the mid-sixties the writing was on the wall for the services from London-Nottingham-Sheffield. On a bright, spring day in 1966, 16B Colwick allocated LMS Class 5 4-6-0 No 44830 is seen at Rugby GC station with a local passenger train. In August of the same year No 44830 moved to 9F Heaton Mersey. (G.W.Sharpe)

49) The former Great Central Main Line was famous for its fast, express freight and speedy loosed-coupled goods services, until the importance of the line was threatened by Doctor Beeching. In February 1962 one of the fleet of BR Class 9F 2-10-0's based at 16D Annesley No 92093 speeds through Rugby (Central) with a Class 8 goods. After closure of the route, many places like Annesley and Woodford Halse became 'ghost towns'. (G.W.Sharpe)

50) In early 1963 thoughts of closure were still far from the thoughts of the footplate staff who worked at depots like Woodford Halse. In March of this year the fireman of LMS Class 8F 2-8-0 No 48002 keeps alert as his charge trundles along light engine near to its home base. Between January 1957 and withdrawal in September 1966, No 48002 worked from a host of depots as far apart as Hasland, Lostock Hall and Willesden. (G.W.Sharpe)

51) Today, the mass of tracks seen in this photograph have long since disappeared, either regained by 'Mother Nature' or man-made items. In March 1963, LMS Class 5 4-6-0 No 44909, from 2A Rugby, is seconded to power an express through Woodford Halse. A longstanding inmate of Rugby shed, No 44909 took its leave on a permanent basis when it was drafted to 1E Bletchley in January 1965, two and a half years prior to withdrawal. (G.W.Sharpe)

52) From June 1960 to December 1962, though not all at the same time, there were a small number of the Gresley LNER J39 Class 0-6-0's on 2F Woodford Halse's books, Nos 64727, 64742, 64747, 64809, 64875 & 64955. One of them, No 64742 is noted out of steam by the side of the shed on 13th May 1962. One example, No 64747 (withdrawn in December 1962) lingered in store at Woodford Halse from condemnation until October 1964. (P.A.Rowlings)

3) Much of the allocation at 2F Woodford Halse were LMS and LNER orientated, along with a large batch of War Department WD Class 8F 2-8-0's and a smattering of BR Standard Classes and the majority of visitors came from sheds in Nottingham, Sheffield and York. One such 'foreigner' from 50A York, LNER B1 Class 4-6-0 No 61198 resides in a siding at Woodford Halse on 24th May 1964, some thirteen months before the complete closure of the shed. (J.K.Carter)

54) We decamp from the former Great Central Main Line and arrive at Northampton, where, on 20th July 1964, the cheerful driver of LMS Class 3F 'Jinty' 0-6-0T No 47590 looks towards the camera as his steed performs shunting duties. Transferred to 1H Northampton this very same month from 5C Stafford, No 47590 was destined to remain there until a further transfer in September 1965 took it to 5B Crewe (South). (Terry Ward)

55) A visitor to Northampton shed on 7th July 1963, coded 2E on this date, LMS *Jubilee* Class 4-6-0 No 45595 *Southern Rhodesia*, from 5A Crewe (North), simmers near to the coal stage as it awaits its next revenue earning duty. For many years *Southern Rhodesia* was a favourite at 9A Longsight (Manchester) before moving to 5A in July 1959. Taken out of traffic in January 1965 it was cut up by Cashmores, Great Bridge. (Terry Ward)

56) We move further east to Syston South Junction, the junction of lines leading to Trent (northbound) and Melton Mowbray (eastbound), the station of which closed in 1968. In 1958, however, Syston station was still very much open. LMS Class 8F 2-8-0 No 48082, from 18C Hasland, passes the Midland Railway inspired South Junction signalbox with an up goods train. Note the profusion of tracks in the foreground. (A.C.Ingram)

57) The flat countryside at Sileby, between Syston and Loughborough, enabled the Midland Railway engineers to lay their tracks on the level which probably explains why BR Class 9F 2-10-0 No 92159, of 15A Wellingborough, is apparently coasting along with its heavy up Class J freight on 4th June 1962. Like Syston, Sileby lost its local passenger services when the station was axed during 1968. (B.W.L.Brooksbank)

58) The city of Leicester is the venue for the next batch of photographs and on an unknown date in the mid-fifties, a duet of LMS Class 4 'Flying Pig' 2-6-0's assemble coaching stock at Leicester (Midland) station. The nearest locomotive to the camera can be identified as No 43094, an inmate of 31D South Lynn, a depot it was to depart from in February 1959 after closure. No 43094 then found a new home at 31C Kings Lynn. (R.S.Carpenter)

59) Moving across Leicester the next location is at Belgrave Road. A group of assorted enthusiasts gather near to the cab of LMS Class 5 4-6-0 No 45238, from 16A Nottingham, which is being employed on the Railway Correspondence & Travel Society special 'East Midlands Branch Lines Tour' on 18th May 1963. This particular station at Belgrave Road, noted for its holiday traffic to East coast resorts, closed during 1963. (D.Webster)

60) The main depot in Leicester was at Leicester Midland, coded 15C and 15A under British Railways, with a smaller sister shed at Leicester GC which closed in July 1964. Before diesels took over most of the express workings on the former Midland main line, Leicester (Midland) shed had a small allocation of LMS *Jubilee* Class 4-6-0's on its books, but they were gone in December 1963, when LMS Class 8F 2-8-0 No 48105 (16E Kirkby) was noted in steam in the yard. (G.W.Sharpe)

61) 21A Saltley allocated LMS *Jubilee* Class 4-6-0 No 45653 *Barham* looks in fine external fettle, apart from the pile of discarded ash dumped in front of the smokebox, as it rests between duties near to the turntable in April 1963 shortly after being drafted to 21A from 24E Blackpool. Simmering next to *Barham* is one of the fleet of BR Class 9F 2-10-0's allocated to 15A Wellingborough, No 92100. (G.W.Sharpe)

62) The next venue in this East Midlands safari is at Wellingborough on the Midland Main line from Bedford to Kettering. An assortment of buildings and covered roof structures along with a member of the station staff host the arrival of LMS Class 5 4-6-0 No 45308, from 2E Northampton, which is in charge of a short express on 15th May 1963. No 45308 stayed at Northampton shed until closure in September 1965, moving to 2D Banbury. (D.Webster)

63) The gradient post in the left of this photograph informs us that the track is rising at a gentle 1 in 149 as BR Class 9F 2-10-0 No 92154, from the nearby shed at 15A, rattles through Wellingborough station on 15th May 1963. Despite its unkempt external condition, No 92154 survived in revenue earning service until July 1967 from 8C Speke Junction. It was scrapped by Thompsons, of Stockton-on-Tees in January 1968. (D.Webster)

64) Although a large shed with a massive allocation, 15A Wellingborough was a rather unsung place because most of its scheduled services were freight orientated. In numbers, the LMS Class 8F 2-8-0's and BR Class 9F 2-10-0's represented a high proportion of the engines based at Wellingborough. All of the Crosti-boilered 9F's were at 15A at one time or another. This 1958 print shows three of their number 'on shed' including No 92021. (N.E.Preedy)

65) Remaining on the Midland Main line we travel a few miles from Wellingborough, to Market Harborough. A lengthy bridge spans the myriad of tracks as LMS Class 5 4-6-0 No 44716, from 1F Rugby, passes a lofty double semaphore signal post with an express on 11th April 1964. Up until closure in October 1965, Market Harborough boasted a small locoshed coded 2F and then 15F. It lost its parent depot status in October 1960. (T.R.Amos)

66) In steam days the Leicestershire area was known for its reliance on coal as were the neighbouring Counties of Derbyshire, Nottinghamshire, Staffordshire and Warwickshire, but for some, to actually name a place 'Coalville', might well be going over the top. Accompanied by an unidentified sister engine, bedraggled 16A Toton LMS Class 8F 2-8-0 No 48681 is surrounded by fire irons at Coalville shed on 26th February 1964. (N.E.Preedy)

67) Another bastion of steam in the East Midlands area was at Kettering, between Market Harborough and Wellingborough. With steam leaking from many joints, work-stained BR Class 9F 2-10-0 No 92019, allocated to 15A Wellingborough, restarts a loose-coupled freight through Kettering station on 2nd February 1963. Like many other 9F's, No 92019 was destined to end its life at 12A Carlisle (Kingmoor), withdrawn in June 1967. (N.E.Preedy)

68) Virtually every town of any size in this area of England appeared to have its own shed and Kettering was no exception to this general rule. Built and owned by the Midland Railway it carried the codes of 15B and 15C under British Railways ownership. Fire irons, a brazier, ash and other bric-a-brac are to be seen next to former Crosti BR Class 9F 2-10-0 No 92024 (15C Leicester - Midland) on 11th April 1963. (D.Webster)

69) The frail looking coaling structure at Kettering has seen better days in this picture taken on 11th March 1965, where the brickwork is crumbling before our very eyes. The locomotive on view is not exactly in its prime either - a sign of the times. The depot is only three months away from closure and the engine, BR Class 2 2-6-0 No 78027, from 15A Leicester (Midland), has only six months of life left. (D.Webster)

70) We swing away from the east of the region and find ourselves at Hasland shed, some fifty minutes walk from Chesterfield (Midland) station for the intrepid spotter who was on foot. In its hey-day Hasland, coded 18C, hired locomotives out to Clay Cross Works and Williamsthorpe Colliery. A visitor to the depot on 4th October 1959 is LMS Class 4F 0-6-0 No 44586, from 55B Stourton on the North Eastern Region. (N.E.Preedy)

71) A brace of Stanier LMS Class 5 4-6-0's, led by No 45025, allocated to 12B Carlisle (Upperby), speed through Madeley, on the racing ground between Crewe and Stafford, with an express in July 1959. Based at 1A Willesden until the move north to Upperby in July 1958, No 45025 was destined to survive until the end of steam on BR, being condemned from 10A Carnforth in August 1958. Today, Aviemore is the home of No 45025. (M.Paine)

72) Lingering at Madeley briefly, we go back in time some six years, to a sun-filled 22nd July 1953. A rather run-down LMS *Jubilee* Class 4-6-0 No 45596 *Bahamas*, an inhabitant of 8A Edge Hill (Liverpool), unleashes a plume of black smoke as it charges towards the camera with a Birkenhead to Euston express. By coincidence, *Bahamas* shared the same fate as No 45025 in the previous photo, being saved by the preservation movement. (R.W.Hinton)

73) A panoramic view of the north end of Stafford in the late fifties. The lines to the left lead to Shrewsbury and the ones on the right to Uttoxeter and Derby. Both are long gone, as is the locomotive in the frame, LMS *Coronation* Class 4-6-2 No 46253 *City of Salford*, from 5A Crewe (North), which is in charge of an up express from Crewe to London. Note the 'unusual' location for the line of washing in the right of the picture! (G.W.Sharpe)

74) The photographer clicks his shutter and another fine locomotive is recorded for posterity. Displaying the 'Lion on Wheel' logo, soon to be replaced by a more modern one, BR *Britannia* Class 4-6-2 No 70042 *Lord Roberts* is eased out of Stafford with a northbound express in August 1958. *Lord Roberts* has not long been transferred to the LMR from 30A Stratford, being based at 9E Trafford Park in Manchester. (D.K.Jones)

5) Although 5C Stafford shed had a sizeable allocation it did not own any locomotives from the more illustrious named classes of LMS engines. However, the odd 'named' celebrity appeared as a visitor as this picture bears witness to. At rest in Stafford shed yard on an unknown day in 1961 is 5A Crewe (North) LMS *Jubilee* Class 4-6-0 No 45625 *Sarawak* which was withdrawn from active service in August 1963 from 24L Carnforth. (D.K.Jones)

6) Another visitor to Stafford depot, this time during 1960, is LMS Class 4 'Duck Six' 0-6-0 No 44551, from 17B Burton, seen at rest near to the station. The main steam engine classes which were housed at Stafford shed came from the LMS Class 4 2-6-4 Tanks, LMS Class 5 4-6-0's, LMS Class 3F 0-6-0 Tanks, LMS Class 8F 2-8-0's and the LNWR Class 7F 0-8-0's. From February 1960 to May 1960 Stafford had a solitary WD Class 8F 2-8-0 No 90147. (G.W.Sharpe)

77) Another brace of LMS Class 5 4-6-0's are together in tandem, this time in the Trent Valley. 8A Edge Hill (Liverpool) No 44773 is the leading locomotive as the engines and express are captured by the camera at Colwich in July 1959. Colwich, junction of the West Coast Main Line to Crewe and another to Stone and Stoke, lost its station in 1958. Edge Hill lost the services of No 44773 when it was condemned in December 1967. (M.Paine)

78) Badnall Wharf, at Norton Bridge, between Stafford and Crewe, became a dumping ground for redundant steam locomotives in the late fifties prior to them being scrapped. In tandem in an isolated section of the yard at Badnall Wharf are LMS Class 1P 0-4-4T No 58066, late of 55D Royston (withdrawn in October 1958) and LNW Class 2F 0-6-0ST No 51453, withdrawn the same date from 56D Mirfield - photographed on 14th July 1959. (T.R.Amos)

79) We remain in the Trent Valley at Lichfield where two youngsters, the older one in braces, observe the passage of LMS Unrebuilt *Patriot* No 45549, from 12A Carlisle (Upperby), as it heads southwards with a holiday extra in July 1955. There are nine years of life ahead for No 45549 which had spells at 8A Edge Hill (Liverpool) and 8B Warrington prior to being taken out of service from the latter in June 1962. (D.K.Jones)

80) What a difference a decade can make. In the previous picture there is not an overhead electric cable in sight, but on 18th September 1965 the situation is somewhat different. Bright, late summer sunshine envelopes the countryside near to Lichfield (Trent Valley) station as BR Class 9F 2-10-0 No 92153, from 8C Speke Junction, heads a lengthy partially fitted freight in a down direction. (T.R.Amos)

81) We again vacate fomer London & North Western rails and switch to ones once owned by the Midland Railway, this time at Burton-on-Trent, world famous for its Breweries and draught ales. This is a view looking towards Derby. Lurking by one of the platforms is a resident of 21A Saltley LMS Class 5 4-6-0 No 44888 which is in charge of a Derby (Midland) to Birmingham (New Street) local passenger train on 15th March 1958. (F.Hornby)

82) The next photo stop is at Derby itself, once the bastion of Midland Railway steam. On 8th September 1956 LMS Class 4F 0-6-0 No 44163, from 17D Rowsley, plods through with a loose-coupled goods, passing LMS Class 5 4-6-0 No 45129 (10C Patricroft) in the process. There were mixed fortunes ahead for these locos with No 44163 being withdrawn from Rowsley in July 1960 and No 45129 from 8B Warrington six years later. (S.Dartnell)

33) This second photograph, recorded once more on 8th September 1956 by the same photographer, records three former Midland Railway locomotives in harness as light engines next to Derby (Midland) station. At the forefront is Class 1F 0-6-0T No 41847 (withdrawn in March 1960). In the middle is Class 3F 0-6-0T No 47561 (withdrawn in August 1960), followed by Class 1F 0-6-0T No 41724 (withdrawn in June 1958). (S.Dartnell)

34) A gaggle of trainspotters throng the platform at Derby (Midland) on the same day as the previous two prints. The background is filled by buildings of various shapes and sizes, whilst in the foreground the fireman of LMS Class 4P 'Compound' 4-4-0 No 41140 relaxes in his seat in the cab prior to setting off with a local passenger train. Condemned from 17A Derby in May 1957 No 41140 was cut up at Derby Works the same month. (S.Dartnell)

85) This portrait sums up the magic of what it was like within the confines of a mighty roundhouse when steam still ruled. Sheds might have been dirty and dangerous and filled with sulphurous fumes, but to enthusiasts they were almost the epitome of life. On an unknown day in 1964 two LMS Class 8F 2-8-0's are stationed by a turntable at 16C. The one on the left is No 48510, local to Derby shed. (D.K.Jones)

86) Derby shed and Works more or less existed side by side and engines overhauled by the latter were soon returned to the shed in readiness to be steamed and returned to their home depots. LMS Class 0F 0-4-0ST No 47004 looks in fine fettle at Derby shed on 7th June 1953 as it awaits the return journey to 18C Hasland where it was to survive in service until rendered surplus to operating requirements in January 1964. (A.N.H.Glover)

87) Hordes of enthusiasts, mostly youngsters, throng round the showpiece of an open day at Derby Works on 28th August 1965, BR *Britannia* Class 4-6-2 No 70012 *John of Gaunt*, from 5B Crewe (South) and bereft of nameplates. Twenty-nine years on and one wonders what these folk are doing today. We know the fate of *John of Gaunt*, withdrawn from 12A Carlisle (Kingmoor) in December 1967 and cut up by Wards of Beighton, Sheffield. (K.L.Seal)

88) We take our leave of this mighty railway centre and find ourselves at Breadsall, on the line from Derby (Friargate) to Nottingham. On a cold looking 31st January 1965 LMS Class 5 4-6-0 No 44811, of 16C Derby, drifts by the camera tender-first as it heads north with an 'engine and brake'. From January 1957 until condemnation in October 1966, No 44811 was based in the Midlands, at Burton, Leicester, Derby and Colwick. (K.L.Seal)

89) The next venue of the North Midlands itinerary is at Nottingham famous for the days of Robin Hood and the exploits of Brian Clough at Nottingham Forest in later years. Like many major cities Nottingham had two main railway stations: Midland and Victoria. Thanks to the efforts of Doctor Beeching the GC one at Victoria was closed during 1967. In this early 1970's picture an array of signals and some track still survived. (Don Powell)

90) A few months before complete closure the station still echoed to the sounds of steam and on 13th August 1966 LMS Class 8F 2-8-0 No 48197 (16B Colwick) has been spruced up to head the RCTS 'Great Central Railtour' (note 'CLK' on smokebox door). Shortly after hauling this special No 48197 was drafted to Manchester, at 9D Newton Heath. It finished its British Railways career at 9K Bolton, withdrawn in April 1968. (F.Hornby)

91) 16A Nottingham shed possessed a legion of the LMS Class 8F 2-8-0's like No 48286 which threads its way through a section of the city of Nottingham with mineral wagons in August 1962. This particular specimen had been at 16A since July 1958 after a short spell at 21A Saltley. It remained at Nottingham shed until January 1964 when it was moved to 16G Westhouses, a depot it was to die at in September 1966. (G.W.Sharpe)

92) In 1959 Nottingham (Midland) as it was then called to distinguish it from the ex. Great Central railway station, had frequent visits from the local LMS Class 2P 4-4-0's like No 40454 (16A) on 17th April of this year, which is standing light engine near to one of the signalboxes. Modernisation in the form of diesel multiple units consigned engines like No 40454 to the scrapyard in droves soon after their introduction. (Peter Hay)

93) The depot which served Nottingham (Midland) was a massive affair with three roundhouses. At its height it owned a mighty fleet of steam locomotives including LMS *Jubilee* and *Royal Scot* Class 4-6-0's, but on 16th May 1965 its allocation had died or been transferred away. On this date there was just one solitary steam engine to be seen, LMS Class 3F 0-6-0T No 47645 which had been withdrawn the previous month. (N.E.Preedy)

94) On the same date the photographer visited the rival shed at 40E Colwick, which serviced Nottingham (Victoria) and freight services on the former GC lines. Unlike 16A Nottingham (Midland) it had no roundhouses and its large allocation was housed within the large confines of a straight structure. Photographed in front of part of the running shed are two of the locally based WD Class 8F 2-8-0's Nos 90002 and 90545. (N.E.Preedy)

95) Yet another enormous steam depot in the Nottinghamshire area was at Toton, situated between Long Eaton and Stapleford and Sandiacre stations: coded 18A and 16A under BR ownership. Like Nottingham (Midland) it had a number of roundhouses and a massive allocation of steam until closure around the end of 1965. A visitor to Toton on 10th May 1964 is LMS Class 3F 0-6-0T No 47273, from 15B Wellingborough. (N.E.Preedy)

96) Returning briefly to the former Great Central Main Line we espy begrimed and work-stained BR Class 9F 2-10-0 No 92011, allocated to 16B Annesley, near Wilford just south of Nottingham with a northbound freight train on 12th May 1965. At this stage in time Annesley had a large fleet of these engines on its books, but this was soon to change and most were transferred away during 1965 including No 92011. (K.L.Seal)

97) The Cromford and High Peak line, now long defunct, was very famous in its day and access to some sections of the line was all but impossible by road. At one time there were three small sub-sheds, Cromford, Middleton Top and Sheep Pasture which for many years came under the control of 17D Rowsley, later recoded 17C and 16J. In June 1953, North London Class 2F 0-6-0T No 58862 (with a cheery crew) poses at Cromford Wharf. (G.W.Sharpe)

98) On the same day LMS Class 0F 0-4-0ST No 47000 (17D Rowsley) is photographed at Sheep Pasture whilst in charge of wagons filled with intrepid enthusiasts. Situated on the south side of the 'High Peak' line, there was no direct access to Sheep Pasture by public highway which gives some indication of how remote the area is. No 47000 moved on to 'Pastures' new in January 1959, going to 17A Derby. (G.W.Sharpe)

99) A more than bedraggled LMS Class 5 4-6-0 No 44751 (8C Speke Junction) fitted with Caprotti valve gear and Timken roller bearings is only four months away from condemnation as it heads a lengthy mixed freight through Rowsley station in the heart of the Peak District on Saturday, 16th May 1964. This former Midland Railway station, situated between Chinley and Matlock fared little better than No 44751, closing in 1967. (J.D.Gomersall)

100) Another engine type which worked over the Cromford and High Peak Railway was from the ranks of the LNER J94 Class 0-6-0 Saddle Tanks, Nos 68006/12/13/30/34/68/79, though not all at the same time. All were based at Rowsley shed which, like the station, also closed in 1967. In the shed yard on 29th July 1962 is No 68006. Rowsley had a rough deal in railway terms, losing its station, shed and freight yards in the sixties. (J.Schatz)

101) We venture a few miles from Rowsley to Hasland in the vicinity of Clay Cross and pause at the shed, coded 18C, which at one time housed a large proportion of the Beyer-Garratt 2-6-6-2 Tanks. Inside the 'open roundhouse' on 4th October 1959 are two well cleaned LMS Fowler Class 4 2-6-4 Tanks Nos 42326 and 42352 which were allocated briefly to Hasland from July to November 1959. The shed closed in September 1964. (N.E.Preedy)

102) The area around Shirebrook once boasted several sheds including Langwith Junction (closed in February 1966) from which this particular engine WD Class 8F 2-8-0 No 90292 was based from September 1964 until withdrawal in October 1965. Shirebrook had three stations, North (GC) closed in 1955, South (GN) closed in 1931 and West (MID) closed in 1964. No 90292 is noted at Shirebrook North with two brakevans on 15th May 1965. (A.R.Curtis)

(03) Another location in the area which once had two locomotive depots was at Staveley. Both closed their doors to steam during 1965. The GC shed closed completely on 14th June with Barrow Hill following suit on 4th October (to steam only). Still displaying its former LMS ownership Class 3F 0-6-0 No 43224 rests outside the roundhouse at 18D Barrow Hill on 15th October 1950. It was withdrawn from the shed in November 1957. (A.N.H.Glover)

(04) We swing away from Staveley to the final location in this chapter, to 5F Uttoxeter, still famed for its racecourse. This was an unsung shed basically in the middle of nowhere in railway terms. The little three road shed only ever had a small allocation and closed for ever on 7th December 1964. Noted at the depot on 9th September 1962 are two LMS Class 4 2-6-4 Tanks Nos 42663 and 42454 along with LMS Class 6P5F 2-6-0 No 42926 (5D Stoke). (T.R.Amos)

CHAPTER FOUR - SOUTH MIDLANDS

105) We switch to the south of the region and turn our attentions to the magnificent city of Gloucester which at its height had two
stations and two motive power depots. On 4th August 1964 there are signals galore at Tramway Junction as 16B Annesley
LMS Class 5 4-6-0 No 44847 powers a holiday express past the camera. It was extremely rare to see a locomotive from
Annesley in the Gloucester area. (J.K.Carter)

06) The raised semaphores in the background signal a clear path ahead for LMS *Jubilee* Class 4-6-0 No 45647 *Sturdee*, from 21A Saltley, as it storms out of Gloucester (Eastgate) with a Leeds to Bristol express on 7th June 1963. The footplate crew are keen to be included in the photograph as they lean out of the cab. An LMR based engine for many years, *Sturdee* finished its working life at sheds on the North Eastern Region. (N.E.Preedy)

07) Gloucester as viewed from the Birmingham direction. In the right of the frame is Horton Road shed (85B). A double-headed Bristol (Temple Meads) to York express approaches with BR Class 5 4-6-0 No 73018 (82C Swindon) leading. Trailing behind is LMS *Jubilee* Class 4-6-0 No 45663 *Jervis*, from 22A Bristol Barrow Road. No 73018 appears to be doing all the work as they pass Tramway Junction in October 1955. (N.E.Preedy)

108) Now a station of the past, Gloucester (Eastgate) pays host to LMS *Jubilee* Class 4-6-0 No 45682 *Trafalgar* (82E Bristol Barrow Road) as it awaits departure with a northbound Bristol (Temple Meads) to Birmingham (New Street) express on 15th March 1960. Ahead lies a fast stretch through Worcestershire and the formidable Lickey Incline. Eastgate station, of Midland Railway vintage, closed to passengers during 1975. (Tim Farebrother)

109) A fine panoramic view of the railway scene at Gloucester as taken from a platform at the Birmingham end of Eastgate station in June 1961. GWR *Castle* Class 4-6-0 No 4092 *Dunraven Castle* has just passed over Tramway Crossing and enters Eastgate with a Wolverhampton (Low Level) to Paignton service. Horton Road depot is on the left and the Midland goods yard containing LMS Class 3F 0-6-0T No 47417 (85C Barnwood) is on the right. (N.E.Preedy)

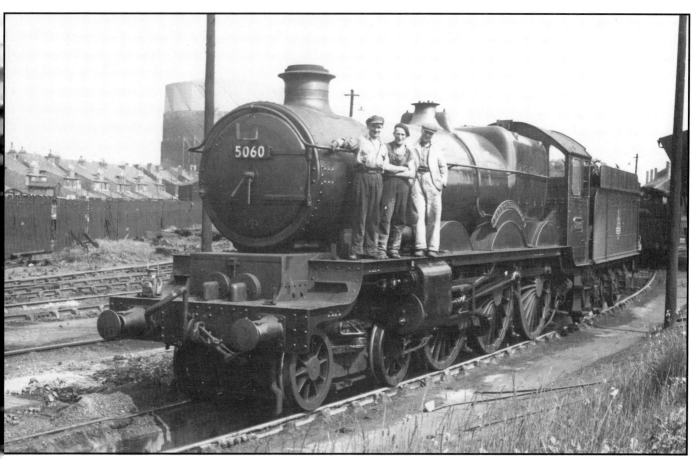

110) A trio of members of the shed staff at 85B Gloucester (Horton Road) pose in bright sunshine for their photograph to be taken on the running plate of visiting GWR *Castle* Class 4-6-0 No 5060 *Earl of Berkeley*, from 81A Old Oak Common, on 3rd June 1951. The houses in Great Western Road remain with us today, as does the gasholder, but all else has gone, including No 5060, withdrawn from Old Oak in April 1963. (N.E.Preedy)

11) We move a short distance to the former Midland Railway depot at Barnwood, coded 22B, 85E and 85C under British Railways. Positioned within the roundhouse the photographer captures the scene outside where spotters on a railtour mill around the yard. The focus of attention in the distance is LMS Class 4F 0-6-0 No 44167 a Barnwood inmate on the day of the visit -12th August 1960. The depot closed officially on 10th May 1964. (D.K.Jones)

112) We travel towards Birmingham on the main line from Gloucester and dwell awhile at Cheltenham where the Midland and Great Western lines once split and went their different routes to Birmingham. In March 1961 GWR *Castle* Class 4-6-0 No 7026 *Tenby Castle*, from 84A Wolverhampton (Stafford Road), passes Malvern Road station (closed in 1966) with X07 a return excursion to Paddington from Cheltenham Racecourse on Gold Cup Day. (N.E.Preedy)

113) The rival station to Malvern Road is at Lansdowne, former Midland Railway, and is still with us today. On 26th May 1958 it is invaded by a locomotive of Great Western design, which was constructed by BR at Swindon Works. Steam leaks from many outlets as *Modified Hall* Class 4-6-0 No 7902 *Eaton Mascot Hall*, from far off 81A Old Oak Common, is unusually employed on a Gloucester to Birmingham stopping passenger train. (N.E.Preedy)

14) In addition to Lansdowne and Malvern Road there was a third station at Cheltenham in BR days, at St. James which closed in the same year as Malvern Road. To supply the local needs of the three stations there was a small shed situated adjacent to Malvern Road. For many years it was a sub-shed to 85B Gloucester (Horton Road) until closure in October 1963. On shed on 4th April 1958 is GWR 1400 Class 0-4-2T No 1401 (85B). (N.E.Preedy)

15) LMS Fowler designed Class 4F 0-6-0 No 44203, from 21A Saltley, heads northwards through Defford (closed in 1965) on the main line from Cheltenham to Bromsgrove, with a mixed freight on 14th May 1960. Being a Saturday, there was much traffic on this busy line and the upper quadrants were in constant use. Engines like No 44203 were very common on this route on both freight and passenger services alike until about 1964. (Tim Farebrother)

116) During the summer of 1962 it was the eleventh hour for the mighty GWR *King* Class 4-6-0's and enthusiasts and photographers alike turned out to record the last rites on the Paddington to Birkenhead services. One such photographer is captured on film as he clicks the shutter to record the storming of Hatton Bank by No 6022 *King Edward III* (84A Wolverhampton - Stafford Road) with a down express on 8th September 1962. (J.Downing)

117) Lingering at Hatton station the up loop is occupied by Churchward GWR 2800 Class 2-8-0 No 3842, from far away 86C Cardiff (Canton), which is awaiting a passage between trains to continue its southbound journey in June 1960 with a Class 8 goods. Later this same month No 3842 was transferred to 86G Pontypool Road. Future homes for this engine were at Oxley, St.Philips Marsh, Swindon and Severn Tunnel Junction. (L.C.Jacks)

118) For many years there were four tracks between Tyseley and Lapworth on the main line to Paddington, but now sadly they are down to two due in the main to the drop in traffic and the downgrading of the route. On 14th October 1962 one of the four tracks at Lapworth is occupied by GWR *Castle* Class 4-6-0 No 7015 *Carn Brea Castle*, of 81A Old Oak Common, which has paused briefly with an unidentified express. (R.W.Hinton)

119) Of the thirty members of the illustrious GWR *King* Class 4-6-0's, three are thankfully preserved today. One of the trio, No 6024 *King Edward I*, again from 81A Old Oak Common, is recorded at Warwick with an express on 7th June 1960. Condemned from 88A Cardiff (Canton) in June 1962, No 6024 lay in storage at Cardiff, Swindon and Barry Docks until approximately April 1973. It is now actively preserved at Quainton Road. (N.E.Preedy)

120) Moving a short distance from Warwick the next location is at Leamington Spa. Fresh from Swindon Works 81F Oxford based GWR *Hall* Class 4-6-0 No 6924 *Grantley Hall* throws out a black pall of smoke from its funnel and blows off excess steam whilst taking refreshment from the adjacent water column on an up passenger in the fifties. The rival to the GWR General station, Leamington Spa Avenue, closed during 1965. (R.S.Carpenter)

121) The flagship of the fleet, pioneer engine of the *King* Class 4-6-0's No 6000 *King George V* a longstanding inmate of 81A Old Oak Common, stands silently at Leamington Spa General with a Birkenhead to Paddington express on 4th June 1960. Although 'officially' preserved after being taken out of service in December 1962 *King George V* lay stored and unwanted for many years at Swindon Works and 30A Stratford before being restored by Bulmers, Hereford. (D.K.Jones)

122) Until its complete closure on 14th June 1965 Leamington had its own shed, coded 84D and later 2L which supplied locomotives for local needs. It also supplied bankers for the North Warwick line after Stratford-upon-Avon shed closed in September 1962. Much of the allocation at Leamington were of the tank engine variety like GWR 5100 Class 2-6-4T No 4118 and GWR 8100 Class 2-6-2T No 8100 on 18th February 1962. (D.Harrison)

123) Nowadays Paddington bound trains go from Birmingham (New Street) via Birmingham International and Coventry to Leamington diesel hauled, a far cry from the days when the majestic *Kings* departed on the direct route from Birmingham (Snow Hill). Coventry also had a steam depot which closed in situ on 16th November 1958 coded 2D. Four and a half years before closure ex. MR Class 2F 0-6-0 No 58293 is seen on 25th April 1954. (N.E.Preedy)

124) Another important staging post on the Paddington to Birmingham route is at Banbury, much reduced in importance today with its links to the former Great Central Main Line from Marylebone to Nottingham and the line to Towcester long since severed. Empty cattle trucks are parked in sidings in the left of this picture as GWR *Hall* Class 4-6-0 No 6906 *Chicheley Hall*, a local engine, stands at signals on 4th August 1964. (D.K.Jones)

125) A general view of Banbury station looking south on a murky 21st May 1960. In the foreground LNER L1 Class 2-6-4T No 67743, from 2F Woodford Halse, arrives with a local passenger train from Woodford. Note the modern post-war buildings which still survive today. There are goods loops on the left and a Western Region local train is in a bay on the right. Three months after this picture was taken No 67743 moved to 9G Gorton. (F.Hornby)

126) Banbury shed, coded 84C under the Western Region and 2D after the London Midland Region took over, was situated to the south of Banbury station and it opened on 6th October 1908. It was of standard straight construction with brick walls and a slated roof. On an unknown day in 1959 GWR *Modified Hall* Class 4-6-0 No 7911 *Lady Margaret Hall*, a visitor to Banbury shed from 81F Oxford, prepares to take on fresh coal supplies. (D.K.Jones)

127) Even before 1966 the London Midland authorities had gradually replaced Great Western types at most of the former Western Region sheds it inherited in the early sixties. By 22nd July 1966 the allocation at Banbury was a mixture of LMS and BR types like LMS Class 5 4-6-0 No 44865, from 2A Tyseley. The shed closed its doors to steam some fifty-eight years to the day after it opened, on 3rd October 1966. (D.Oakes)

128) We now move to the extreme south of the Midlands, to the university city of Oxford. GWR *Castle* Class 4-6-0 No 5071 *Spitfire* (85A Worcester) prepares to leave its train on 22nd August 1959 and hand it over to a SR *Lord Nelson* Class 4-6-0 for the run to the south coast via Basingstoke. No 5071 was renamed *Spitfire* for propaganda reasons in September 1940, losing its original name of *Clifford Castle* (applied later to No 5098). (N.L.Browne)

129) A large water tank and an array of lower quadrant semaphores dominate the left side of this picture as GWR *Hall* Class 4-6-0 No 6953 *Leighton Hall*, a longstanding resident of 81D Reading, arrives at Oxford on a sun-filled 10th August 1963 with a Margate to Wolverhampton (Low Level) service which has come via Redhill and Guildford. *Leighton Hall* finally took its leave of Reading shed in January 1965, moving to 81E Didcot. (A.F.Nisbet)

30) As a direct contrast to the previous picture it is dull and cold at Oxford on 5th November 1963. Almost at the end of its career, 81A Old Oak Common GWR *Castle* Class 4-6-0 No 5057 *Earl Waldergrave* waits with an express as a railwayman looks on as parcels are loaded onto the train. Condemned four months later from Old Oak in March 1964, *Earl Waldergrave* was scrapped at its birthplace, Swindon in August of the same year. (J.K.Carter)

31) Looking in pristine condition after overhaul at Swindon Works, GWR *Hall* Class 4-6-0 No 5979 *Cruckton Hall*, another longstanding resident of 81D Reading, threads a path through Oxford station on a partially fitted goods train in 1962. In March 1963 *Cruckton Hall* departed from Reading shed for good, transferring to 85B Gloucester (Horton Road). A final transfer took it to 85A Worcester in October 1964. (D.Webster)

132) Being as Oxford was such an important station and a change-over point for steam locomotives it is not surprising that it had its own locoshed, but what is amazing is its construction of wood as can be clearly seen in this print of 22nd June 1962. From left to right are GWR 2800 Class 2-8-0 No 3827 (86A Newport - Ebbw Junction), BR Class 4 4-6-0 No 75028 (1E Bletchley) and GWR *Castle* Class 4-6-0 No 5057 *Earl Waldergrave* (81A Old Oak Common). (J.Schatz)

133) Sunlight and shadows in the yard at 81F Oxford on 8th March 1964. GWR *Hall* Class 4-6-0 No 5955 *Garth Hall*, a local resident in filthy condition, towers over the photographer. Next to *Garth Hall*, in an equally forlorn state is sister engine No 6935 *Browsholme Hall*, from 86B Newport (Ebbw Junction). For English spotters *Garth Hall* was an elusive beast being shedded at 87E Landore until drafted to 81F in November 1960. (J.K.Carter)

34) To augment its predominantly Great Western allocation a number of BR Class 4 4-6-0's were based at Oxford shed, Nos 75000/1/7/8/21/22/24/27/29, though not all at the same time. One example, fitted with a double chimney (September 1962), No 75008 stands dead in the yard in May 1963. Once of 86C Cardiff (Canton) No 75008 arrived at 81F in October 1958. It served from here until July 1964, moving to 83G Templecombe. (D.K.Jones)

35) Being a cosmopolitan depot Oxford had visitations from sheds of different regions and was a paradise for lovers of steam in those heady days of long ago. Looking in ex. works condition LNER K3 Class 2-6-0 No 61880, from 31A Cambridge, poses for the camera in bright sunshine on 19th March 1961. Surviving until the end of steam on the Western Region 81F became a dumping ground for unwanted locos during 1965. (A.N.H.Glover)

136) A few miles to the north of Oxford is Wolvercote Junction and on 4th June 1963 GWR *Hall* Class 4-6-0 No 6910 *Gossington Hall*, another 81F Oxford engine, speeds by with a fitted freight. Between January 1957 and condemnation in October 1965, *Gossington Hall* spent this period being shuffled back and forth from 81E Didcot and 81F Oxford. Stored at 81F until January 1966 it was cut up by Birds, Risca the following month. (N.E.Preedy)

137) Originally opened in 1873 by the Great Western Railway the little station in the quiet backwater of Witney on the Oxford to Fairford branch is almost at the end of its life on 16th June 1962. On the far platform a little boy appears disinterested in the presence of 81F Oxford based GWR 5700 Class 0-6-0PT No 9654 which is taking water from the nearby column prior to continuing its journey to Fairford. (D.Webster)

(38) The final brace of photographs taken in the South Midlands are centred on Fairford terminus on the lengthy branch line from Oxford which closed completely in 1962. It even had its own turntable, small shed and coaling facilities. On 27th May 1961 a less than clean GWR 2251 Class 0-6-0 No 2221, from 81E Didcot, is in charge of an Oxford bound service. Note the small signalbox at the end of the platform. (Peter Hay)

39) The short platform is deserted at Fairford on the same day as another filthy locomotive, GWR 7400 Class 0-6-0PT No 7445 (81F Oxford) awaits departure. When the branch was shut down the stations at Fairford, Lechlade, Kelmscott and Langford, Alvescot, Carterton, Brize Norton and Bampton, Witney, South Leigh, Eynsham and Cassington Halt closed at the same time. Shortly after closure No 7445 was drafted to 87G Carmarthen. (Peter Hay)

CHAPTER FIVE - WEST MIDLANDS

140) This final chapter is devoted to the West Midlands. With permanent way workers in the distance LMS Class 8F 2-8-0 No 48332, from 16F Burton, ploughs past them with a lengthy empty stock working near Stourbridge on 22nd July 1964. By this stage in time the area was firmly in the grip of the London Midland Region authorities and more and more locomotives like No 48332 were appearing on the scene. (T.R.Amos)

141) We return to happier times when Great Western engines dominated the railway at Stourbridge. On 1st November 1959, a Sunday, some inhabitants of 84F Stourbridge stand inside the roundhouse resting by the turntable. Both GWR 5600 Class 0-6-2 Tanks Nos. 6604 and 6609 began their lives in September 1927 and GWR 5700 Class 0-6-0PT No 8704 in February 1931. No 8704 was withdrawn three months later in February 1960, one of the first 87XX casualties. (Tim Farebrother)

142) Six years earlier on 14th June 1953 two Churchward freight locomotives simmer side by side in the shed yard at 84F along with a GWR railcar. Nearest the camera in light steam is GWR 2800 Class 2-8-0 No 2824 from far away 87F Llanelly. Next to No 2824 is Stourbridge based GWR 2800 Class 2-8-0 No 3821. The former locomotive was gone by August 1959, but No 3821 survived in revenue earning service until October 1964. (N.E.Preedy)

143) We swing east from Stourbridge and alight at Bescot Junction on the indirect route from Birmingham (New Street) to Wolverhampton (High Level). Sporting a stained surround to its smokebox door LMS *Coronation* Class 4-6-2 No 46240 *City of Coventry*, from 1B Camden, heads a diverted express on 9th August 1963. Later this same month *City of Coventry* was ousted from Camden shed and transferred across London to 1A Willesden. (T.R.Amos)

144) Although Bescot shed, coded 3A, 21B and 2F after nationisation, closed to steam on 28th March 1966, the running shed still survives today, though out of use. On 1st August 1965 the yard was packed with steam. Amidst their ranks are LMS Class 4 2-6-0 No 43002, LMS Class 5 4-6-0 No 44839 (16F Burton), LMS Class 2 2-6-0 No 46425, LMS Class 8F 2-8-0 No 48081 (1A Willesden) LMS Class 4 2-6-0 No 43005 and LMS Class 5 4-6-0 No 44843 (2B Oxley) (T.R.Amos)

45) Covered in a white, powdery looking substance, LMS *Jubilee* Class 4-6-0 No 45670 *Howard of Effingham*, a 2A Rugby locomotive, passes through a barren landscape at Bloomfield Junction in the Black Country, with a Manchester to Birmingham (New Street) express in the summer of 1963. Allocated to Rugby shed from January 1961 to December 1963, No 45670 was then sent to 16C Derby and thence to 9B Stockport in September 1964. (L.Brownhill)

46) Under clear signals LMS Class 5 4-6-0 No 44840, from 21B Bescot, steams through the former London & North Western station at Tipton, between Coseley and Dudley Port, and passes the compact signalbox with an express in August 1962. During the last three years of its working life No 44840 served at 2D Banbury, 6A Chester, 5D Stoke and 8H Birkenhead before being withdrawn from the latter in November 1967. (L.Brownhill)

147) Dudley (Joint GWR/LNWR) is the next port of call on a rain-soaked 28th July 1962. A porter chats to the driver of GWR 5100 Class 2-6-2T No 4168 (84F Stourbridge) as it awaits departure with the three coach 10.48am Stourbridge Junction to Wolverhampton (Low Level) local passenger. A small boy leans out of the leading carriage as another porter struggles with a large box in the distance. Closure came in 1964. (J.M.Tolson)

148) Compact terraced houses provide a backcloth for this 1957 photograph of Wednesbury (LNWR) station as LMS Class 2 2-6-2T No 41223, from 3C Walsall, is photographed on the 'Walsall Motor'. Wednesbury (LNWR) was officially named Wednesbury Town despite the WEDNESBURY station board affixed to the fencing on the left. Situated on the Stourbridge to Walsall line it became another closure statistic during 1964. (R.S.Carpenter)

49) Sporting the train reporting number of 048, 81D Reading GWR *Castle* Class 4-6-0 No 5018 *St. Mawes Castle* speeds past Monmore Green and approaches Priestfield station on the GWR main line from Wolverhampton (Low Level) to Birmingham (Snow Hill) with an express on 7th September 1962 two days before the end of the summer timetable. Tucked into a siding on the right is GWR *Modified Hall* Class 4-6-0 No 7929 *Wyke Hall* (84E Tyseley). (T.R.Amos)

50) With the driver perched comfortably in his cab, BR Class 9F 2-10-0 No 92224, from 2D Banbury and equipped with a double chimney, charges through West Bromwich (GWR) with an up fitted freight bound for Birmingham and beyond on 31st July 1965. Introduced into service in June 1958 No 92224 had a working life of only nine years or so before being taken prematurely out of traffic from 8B Warrington in September 1967. (T.R.Amos)

151) Wolverhampton (Low Level) sadly closed its doors to passengers in 1972 after the closure of the former Great Western main line to Birmingham (Snow Hill). In happier times during the summer of 1963 GWR *Castle* Class 4-6-0 No 7034 *Ince Castle*, from 85B Gloucester (Horton Road), sets off with an express. Equipped with a double chimney in December 1959, *Ince Castle* was finally withdrawn from Horton Road in June 1965. (D.K.Jones)

152) During the sixties, before overhead electrification, the express passenger services between Wolverhampton (High Level) and Birmingham (New Street) were shared between steam and diesel locomotives. On 14th October 1960 LMS Unrebuilt *Patriot* Class 4-6-0 No 45503 *The Royal Leicestershire Regiment*, allocated to 24L Carnforth, leaves the High Level station with an express, the first two carriages being of Gresley design. (D.K.Jones)

153) At its height 84A Wolverhampton (Stafford Road) had five different shed buildings, three of which were roundhouses along with two straight structures. In later years two of the roundhouses fell into disrepair and were little used. Fresh from overhaul on 12th October 1952, probably from the nearby Wolverhampton Works, GWR 1400 Class 0-4-2T No 1424, from 85B Gloucester (Horton Road), poses on an open turntable. (B.K.B.Green)

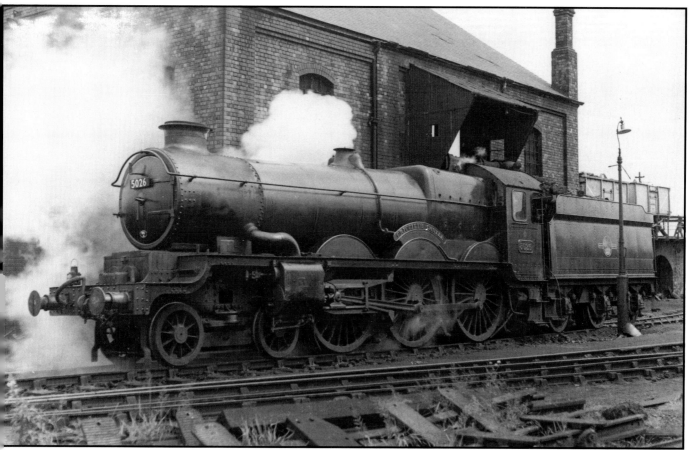

54) Pride of place amongst the allocation at Stafford Road went first and foremost to the GWR *King* Class 4-6-0's. Following on in second place were the GWR *Castle* Class 4-6-0's and many of their number remained at Stafford Road for many years. One such locomotive is No 5026 *Criccieth Castle* seen by the coaling plant in 1962. It was at 84A from April 1958 until closure of the shed in September 1963, moving to nearby Oxley. (R.S.Carpenter)

155) The mainstays of the LMR services from Wolverhampton (High Level) to Birmingham (New Street) came from the ranks of the LMS *Patriot*, *Jubilee* and *Royal Scot* classes. From time to time during the early sixties these were complimented by the use of LMS *Coronation* Class 4-6-2's. At the Wolverhampton end they were serviced at Bushbury shed. On a snowy winter's day in 1962, No 46248 *City of Leeds* (5A Crewe - North) is at the depot. (R.S.Carpenter)

156) In steam days there was a third depot at Wolverhampton, this being at Oxley (coded 84B and 2B). It was situated on the west of the main line which ran north from Wolverhampton (Low Level). On Christmas Eve in 1966 it had lost all of its former allocation of Great Western types and LMR and BR locos had replaced them. In steam in the yard are LMS Class 5 4-6-0 No 44776 (6C Croes Newydd) and BR Class 9F 2-10-0 No 92105 (8H Birkenhead) (Mike Wood)

157) Oxley shed was opened by the Great Western in July 1907 and consisted of two roundhouses within the same roof and a large yard. The nearest station was Dunstall Park (closed in 1968) which provided passengers for the nearby racecourse. The shed closed on 6th March 1967 and the remainder of its working engines were transferred to other depots on the LMR. In the yard in 1949 is GWR Churchward 4300 Class 2-6-0 No 5300. (R.S.Carpenter)

158) A nearby crane lifts its jib in salute to a veteran steam locomotive at Walsall in 1953. With the fireman looking towards the camera Johnson Midland Class 2P (483 Class) 4-4-0 No 40501 (3C Walsall) heads a train in the 'Engineers Sidings'. Built at Derby Works in 1897, No 40501 was rebuilt by Deeley (1904) and Fowler (1912). It was drafted to 22A Bristol Barrow Road in December 1957 and withdrawn in August 1960. (R.S.Carpenter)

159) Moving to the north-west of the region we pause at Wellington (Salop). On a bright, sunny day on 3rd June 1952 GWR *Hall* Class 4-6-0 No 6956 *Mottram Hall*, from 84A Wolverhampton (Stafford Road), has steam to spare as it departs with an up express and passes the locoshed on the right. Before condemnation in December 1965 *Mottram Hall* also served at Shrewsbury, Oxford (twice), Stourbridge and Gloucester (Horton Road) sheds. (B.K.B.Green)

160) The small three road shed at Wellington looks a little fragile on a gloomy and misty 23rd April 1955. In light steam in front of the depot is GWR 5100 Class 2-6-2T No 5178. Hiding within the depths is GWR 1600 Class 0-6-0PT No 1663. Later in life these engines were split by hundreds of miles, No 5178 ending up at 83A Newton Abbot and No 1663 at 6C Croes Newydd. Wellington shed closed on 10th August 1964. (B.K.B.Green)

161) Our next photo-stop is at Shrewsbury. Although predominantly a sanctuary for former Great Western locomotives many London Midland and BR Standard types were to be seen here. On an unknown date in the fifties LMS Unrebuilt *Patriot* Class 4-6-0 No 45544, from 8A Edge Hill (Liverpool), finds itself employed on a local passenger working at Shrewsbury. No 45544 was one of several members of the *Patriot* class which were un-named. (G.W.Sharpe)

162) A member of the footplate crew relaxes in the cab as his charge, LMS *Jubilee* Class 4-6-0 No 45660 *Rooke*, a local engine from the nearby shed at 89A, simmers and sizzles as it awaits uncoupling from the freight train which it has brought in to Shrewsbury from the north on 2nd August 1963. *Rooke* served from sheds on three regions from the late fifties until withdrawal in June 1966: the LMR, WR and NER. (K.L.Seal)

163) To the non railway enthusiast it would be hard to convince him that both of these engines photographed in harness in the yard at Shrewsbury shed are basically from the same stock, despite their vast differences in appearance. LMS Rebuilt *Patriot* Class 4-6-0 No 45525 *Colwyn Bay*, of 1A Willesden, teams up with an unidentified LMS Unrebuilt *Patriot* Class 4-6-0 on the same track on a gloomy day in March 1961. (G.W.Sharpe)

164) During its British Railways days Shrewsbury was coded 84G, 89A and 6D prior to closure in early March 1967. During 1961 it was 89A and on an unknown day it hosts a visiting famous engine from 83A Newton Abbot in the shape of GWR *Castle* Class 4-6-0 No 4037 *The South Wales Borderers*. To the right of No 4037 is a double chimney version of the class, No 7015 *Carn Brea Castle*, one of a number allocated to Shrewsbury. (D.K.Jones)

165) We move many miles across country to the southern section of the West Midlands in Worcestershire to the famous (infamous) Lickey Incline. On 25th August 1962 LMS *Jubilee* Class 4-6-0 No 45576 *Bombay*, from 41A Sheffield (Darnall), attacks the gradient as it leaves Bromsgrove with the 12.13pm express from Gloucester to Newcastle. Looking at the external condition of *Bombay* it is not surprising it was withdrawn four months later. (R.Picton)

166) In 1925 LNER Beyer-Garratt Class 2-8-0 + 0-8-2 No 69999 was the largest and most powerful locomotive in Great Britain with a tractive effort of 72,940 lbs. No 69999 was built for use as a banker on the 1 in 40 gradient from Wentworth Junction to West Silkstone. When the line was electrified it was transferred to Bromsgrove for use on the Lickey Incline. It is shown here on shed at Bromsgrove on 26th March 1949. (A.N.H.Glover)

167) The next four prints concentrate on Worcester, bastion of Great Western steam and one of the last Western Region centres to provide steam power on expresses to and from Paddington. GWR *Grange* Class 4-6-0 No 6817 *Gwenddwr Grange*, a local engine from 85A, looks sadly neglected as it enters Worcester (Shrub Hill) from the north with a local passenger, minus its safety valve bonnet on an unknown day in 1962. (Tim Farebrother)

168) Another GWR *Grange* Class 4-6-0 No 6821 *Leaton Grange* eases a freight past Worcester shed in May 1964. Introduced into service in January 1937 *Leaton Grange* began its life in Cardiff. When photographed it was allocated to 82B St.Philips Marsh, but when 82B closed in June 1964 it moved across Bristol to 82E Barrow Road. Its final home was at 87F Llanelly where it was made surplus to requirements in November 1964. (Tim Farebrother)

69) As previously stated on the opposite page Worcester was possibly the last major centre to provide steam engines on a regular basis to Paddington and back on expresses. Most of the locomotives used were from the diminishing ranks of the GWR *Castle* Class 4-6-0's. For a brief period of time No 5091 *Cleeve Abbey* was allocated to 85A, from April to June 1964, and is photographed outside the shed in May of this year. (Tim Farebrother)

70) The staff at Worcester shed normally took great pride in the outwards appearance of its *Castles* as demonstrated by Nos 7005 *Sir Edward Elgar* and 7011 *Banbury Castle* in 1962. *Sir Edward Elgar*, built in June 1946, spent all of its working life at Worcester, being withdrawn from there in September 1964. *Banbury Castle* survived a little longer, being condemned from 2B Oxley (Wolverhampton) in February 1965. (Tim Farebrother)

171) We remain in the Worcestershire area and move away from Worcester itself to the countryside. GWR *Grange* Class 4-6-0 No 6807 *Birchwood Grange*, another 85A Worcester engine, makes light of a four coach express from Worcester to Hereford near to Great Malvern in 1957. Worcester shed seemed to make a habit of hanging on to its locomotives and *Birchwood Grange* is no exception until it was no longer required in December 1963. (A.C.Ingram)

172) In 1960 Collett GWR 2800 Class 2-8-0 No 3827, from 86A Newport (Ebbw Junction), built during the Second World War in 1940, trundles gently down the bank from Colwall Tunnel, near Malvern Wells, and on towards Worcester with a mixed freight. In November 1962 No 3827 was the first representative of the 38XX series to be condemned (from 86A). The following month it was cut up at its birthplace, Swindon Works. (Tim Farebrother)

73) We switch counties and meander into Herefordshire. GWR *Hall* Class 4-6-0 No 6939 *Calveley Hall*, from 86C Cardiff (Canton), drifts light engine into Hereford station on 25th May 1957. Note the straight-sided tender and the lamp affixed in the local passenger position at the top of the smokebox door. *Calveley Hall* was destined to remain in the Cardiff area until its demise from 88A Cardiff East Dock in October 1963. (N.L.Browne)

74) For spotters going by train to Hereford it was very frustrating for one could not see the occupants of the shed unless one was fortunate enough to travel on the avoiding line. For those on foot it was a 25 minute walk from Hereford station. On 26th April 1964 the depot, coded 86C, is the subject of a shed visit by enthusiasts. At the forefront is 86C based GWR 5100 Class 2-6-2T No 4107 which has just over one year left to live. (Tim Farebrother)

175) We complete this album on 'British Railways Steaming Through The Midlands' with a visit to the long defunct branch line from Ashchurch to Upton-on-Severn, once owned and run by the Midland Railway. In the summer of 1961 ex. MR Class 3F 0-6-0 No 43754, from 85C Gloucester (Barnwood), waits to leave Ashchurch with the Upton service consisting of a single coach. The branch used to continue to Malvern but closed in 1953. (Tim Farebrother)

176) Shedded at Gloucester (Barnwood), coded 85E in 1960, LMS Class 3F 'Jinty' 0-6-0T No 47506 is seen with its single coach at Upton-on-Severn waiting to leave for Ashchurch via Ripple and Tewkesbury. As stated in the above picture the services to Malvern ceased in 1953 and Upton-on-Severn became the terminus. The line closed altogether in 1961 and the only station to survive today is at Ripple, now a private house. (Tim Farebrother)